Roman Mythology
A Captivating Guide to Roman Gods, Goddesses, and Mythological Creatures

© **Copyright 2017**

All Rights Reserved. No part of this book may be reproduced in any form without permission in writing from the author. Reviewers may quote brief passages in reviews.

Disclaimer: No part of this publication may be reproduced or transmitted in any form or by any means, mechanical or electronic, including photocopying or recording, or by any information storage and retrieval system, or transmitted by email without permission in writing from the publisher.

While all attempts have been made to verify the information provided in this publication, neither the author nor the publisher assumes any responsibility for errors, omissions, or contrary interpretations of the subject matter herein.

This book is for entertainment purposes only. The views expressed are those of the author alone, and should not be taken as expert instruction or commands. The reader is responsible for his or her own actions.

Adherence to all applicable laws and regulations, including international, federal, state and local laws governing professional licensing, business practices, advertising, and all other aspects of doing business in the US, Canada, UK, or any other jurisdiction is the sole responsibility of the purchaser or reader.

Neither the author nor the publisher assumes any responsibility or liability whatsoever on behalf of the purchaser or reader of these materials. Any perceived slight of any individual or organization is purely unintentional.

Contents

FREE BONUS FROM CAPTIVATING HISTORY (AVAILABLE FOR A LIMITED TIME) 4

INTRODUCTION 5

    THE SHAPE OF THINGS TO COME 6

CHAPTER 1 — THE TROJAN CONNECTION 9

    WHAT HISTORY AND AN ANALYSIS OF MYTH TELL US 23

CHAPTER 2 — FOUNDING OF ROME 26

    FROM THE SHE-WOLF TO THE FOUNDING OF A GREAT CITY 37

CHAPTER 3 — PURELY ROMAN GODS 39

CHAPTER 4 — BORROWINGS FROM ETRURIA 50

    FROM RASENNA 53

CHAPTER 5 — INFLUENCE OF THE GREEK PANTHEON 55

    FROM THE GREEKS 57

    LESSER GODS AND GODDESSES 60

    GREEK CREATURES ADOPTED BY THE ROMANS 63

CHAPTER 6 — CELTIC POTPOURRI 68

    ROMAN CONQUESTS OF THE CELTS 71

    OTHER BORROWED GODS 80

CHAPTER 7 — TRUTH BEHIND THE ROMAN GODS 83

CONCLUSION - WHAT WE'VE LEARNED 88

FREE BONUS FROM CAPTIVATING HISTORY (AVAILABLE FOR A LIMITED TIME) 92

Free Bonus from Captivating History (Available for a Limited time)

Hi History Lovers!

Now you have a chance to join our exclusive history list so you can get your first history ebook for free as well as discounts and a potential to get more history books for free! Simply visit the link below to join.

Captivatinghistory.com/ebook

Also, make sure to follow us on:

Twitter: @Captivhistory

Facebook: Captivating History: @captivatinghistory

Introduction

Gravitas was a founding principle of Roman society. Life can be brutal, and the Romans figured out early that guiding one's actions with weightiness or seriousness—or, in today's word—intentionality—was necessary. Using *gravitas* as a guide for life made them exceptionally practical—although not particularly creative. In fact, the Romans were an unimaginative society. The creativity they did employ was greatly borrowed –sometimes forcibly-- from other cultures.

Only a few of their gods were entirely Roman. Because little is written during the early years of Rome, it is difficult to separate their own divinities as opposed to those they appropriated.

Originally, the Romans were farmers. Many of their earliest gods dealt with crops, rain, and their main river—the Tiber.

Gravitas, with its intentionality and practicality, led the Romans to think affinities could be cultivated by making their gods look like those of their neighbors. These affinities made assimilation or conquest much easier. Allowing citizens to keep their religious traditions, a widespread practice among some early civilizations, helped make them more compliant with Roman rule. And if Roman traditions looked like the traditions of the conquered peoples, the subjugated populace would believe they truly belonged to Rome.

Like a modern exercise in building a commercial brand, Roman writers of the first century BC developed stories of

Roman myth and history to manufacture legitimacy for their rulers. Virgil (70–19 BC), for instance, gave Rome its most important work of authority—the *Aeneid*, which told the story of Rome's roots in the Trojan War; they were descended from Trojans, the enemies of the Greeks. We'll take a brief look at the truth of this possibility in "Chapter 4 — Borrowings from Etruria."

The Shape of Things to Come

We will look at many aspects of the Roman gods, goddesses, and mythological creatures. Each of the first six chapters begins with a narrative scene which helps bring the legendary and mythical characters to life.

In chapter 1, we explore the seeds of legitimacy that Virgil planted regarding the Trojan connection to Rome. Though Aeneas was a minor character in Homer's epic *Iliad,* Virgil shows Aeneas to be the epitome of what a good Roman should be—heroic, serious, virtuous, and devoted. And, important to the *Iliad*, Aeneas was one of the sons of Venus or, as she was known to the Greeks, Aphrodite—the goddess of love.

How do we get from a Trojan demigod to the reality of Rome? This is the topic of chapter 2. In this chapter, we explore the foundation of that great city by the semi-divine, wolf-suckled brothers, Romulus and Remus. We also consider the myth of Aeneas's son, Ascanius, who was also known as Iulus—the basis of the name of Julius, and the basis of the Julio-Claudian dynasty of the Roman Empire. Virgil gave the family of Julius Caesar its back-story to make his patron, and Rome's first emperor, Augustus, seem worthier of being a living god.

In chapter 3, we examine the gods of Roman origin as well as Roman mythological creatures.

Chapter 4 focuses on the Etruscan influence on Roman mythology. Latin culture co-opted Minerva as its own, and then gave her the Greek attributes of the goddess Athena.

Perhaps the strongest influence in Roman mythology came from the Greeks. The Greeks were far more creative, and their legends were far richer and more detailed. The Greek influence is the topic of chapter 5. The Greeks had expanded their influence to the southern portion of the Italian peninsula far from the tiny Kingdom of Rome. In the centuries before the Roman Republic, the Greeks had expanded into southern France and eastern Spain.

In chapter 6, we delve into the world of Celtic influence and see how the gods of the Celts were melded with the Roman pantheon in creative ways. What we know about the Celtic pantheon comes from the Romans. The Celts used oral storytelling to record their history for generations.

Finally, in chapter 7, we take a brief look at the potential truths behind the Roman gods, goddesses, and creatures. Every myth had a beginning, and in this chapter, we explore some of the possibilities.

The Romans were builders and innovators in many industries. They took existing resources and shaped them to suit their needs. But they also adopted the creative ideas of others. Over time, the Roman pantheon became increasingly a melting pot of ideas blended into a cultural potpourri.

Chapter 1 — The Trojan Connection

Goddess Juno—Jupiter's queen—looked down upon the ragtag fleet of Trojan ships, led by Aeneas, and she sneered with delight as she thought of sinking them to the bottom of the sea. Juno despised Troy and its people. Petty and immature, like all the gods and goddesses—they lacked the maturity and humility to act wisely.

She hated Troy because of Paris, Prince of Troy, snubbed Juno when he judged who was the most beautiful goddess—between Juno (the Greek Hera), Minerva (Athena) and Venus (Aphrodite).

The dispute began at the wedding of the Greek goddess, Thetis, to King Peleus of Aegina.

One goddess, though, despised the event. Eris, goddess of discord, and daughter of Jupiter and Juno was not being invited because the other gods wanted a peaceful event. Her exclusion angered her. She said, "to the fairest one" and threw a golden apple over the wall and into the party. No one caught the apple, but three goddesses claimed the golden apple as her own—Juno, Minerva, and Venus. To settle the dispute, they asked Jupiter to judge between them.

Understanding the potentially dire consequences of such a task, Jupiter chose a mortal to judge who should own the apple based on the inscription: "to the fairest one." That mortal was the fair-minded Paris, Prince of Troy. Jupiter understandably protected himself by choosing Paris, since the choice would upset the two goddesses not selected—and that hostility might last forever. Jupiter protected his own sanity and safety by transferring the dangerous duty onto an expendable and convenient mortal. Perhaps even wise Minerva did not realize how truly foolish Paris would be to accept such an inherently dangerous task.

After the wedding celebration was over Mercury (Hermes) escorted the three goddesses to Asia Minor—also known as Anatolia, or modern Turkey. There, they bathed in a local spring on Mount Ida, not very far from Troy. After freshening up, they found Paris, sitting on a log under the shade of a mature tree, tending to his flock on the slopes of the mountain. Naturally, the prince was surprised to have the three lovely goddesses present him with this interesting challenge.

At first, the goddesses posed before the honest prince-- Juno, Minerva and finally Venus. But Paris could not decide.

"I'm afraid, my ladies," he said, taking a deep breath before continuing, "that this is an impossible task. You are each incredibly beautiful, and my mind is at an impasse."

"What if we were to show you our full form," asked Venus, "without the visual impediment of the divine clothing we typically wear out of sensible modesty?"

The other two goddesses nodded encouragingly.

Paris smiled. He had seen naked women before and knew the pleasure that came with the sight. In fact, his wife was the beautiful mountain nymph, Oenone. The thought that three major goddesses would willingly bare themselves for his judgment aroused him more than he thought possible.

He spoke cautiously, though. He knew of their power, and he did not want to answer rashly and risk offending any of them.

"I can sense the importance of this challenge you've given me. If it pleases each of you that I—a mere mortal—view your beauty in its entirety to complete the charge you've laid upon me, then I will humbly do this thing as you request. I sincerely hope that this will be enough to settle in my own mind an answer to your question."

Again, Juno went first because of her seniority amongst the three goddesses. Quietly, she unfastened her garment and let it fall to her feet. Slowly, she stepped out of it and moved toward the young man as he remained seated.

Closer she came, slowly advancing. When she was close enough to touch, she showed the young man her neck and breasts down to her abdomen. She showed him her thighs and buttocks, as well as the small of her back. As she displayed her physical form in all its splendor, she whispered to him, bribing him in exchange for his vote for her. She would give him rule over all of Europe and Asia, and not merely Asia Minor—from Eriu to Yamato—Ireland to Japan.

As Juno returned to her clothes, the other two goddesses guessed what she had done. Each secretly decided to sway the young prince's decision with the best possible bribe they could consider.

Next, Minerva dropped her clothing and approached Paris, equally seductively. Because of her temperament as a warrior and protectress of the homeland, her movements added power and finesse which Juno lacked. Her earthiness left Paris breathless. As Minerva displayed up-close each curve of her beautiful body, she whispered to him that she could make the young prince the wisest and most skilled of all mortals in the art of war. All he would need to do was to choose her as the owner of the golden apple.

Moments later, as Minerva restored her vestments, Venus dropped her gown and stepped forward, turning with a coy seduction that left the young mortal's heart pounding with each step. This was the goddess of love and Paris felt once again the impossibility of this challenge.

Venus promised that if Paris chose her, she would make it possible for him to marry the most beautiful mortal woman in all the world—the already married, Helen, wife of King Menelaus of Sparta.

Assailed by so much feminine charm, the bribe which raked most heavily across his mind was the one that most closely matched the feelings overpowering his mind, body, and soul. Helplessly, he chose Venus and thus sealed the fate of Troy, setting in motion events that would eventually lead to the creation of Rome.

When Helen left her husband to join Paris in Troy, the Greeks banded together to attack the Trojan capital. Why would there be such unity amongst the usually conflicting

Greek city-states? The leaders of those city-states had agreed to that attack.

Helen was so beautiful that almost every king in the Greek kingdoms sought her hand in marriage. Her wise father feared any man he chose for his daughter would soon lose her because the others would continue to fight over her, even after she married. Minerva's wisdom guided him to bind each king to the father's decision by swearing to protect Helen's marriage to whomever she was to be pledged. Only after each king gave his pledge did the father reveal his choice.

Thus, when Helen left her husband, the other Greek kings were duty-bound to go after her—to protect her marriage to Menelaus of Sparta. For a decade, they laid siege to Troy to protect those wedding vows between Menelaus and Helen. In the end, Troy lost, and the city was destroyed.

Now that Juno and Minerva had ensured the collapse of Troy, after its ten-year war against the Greeks, its remaining citizens were dispersed throughout the eastern Mediterranean. The future heritage of Troy depended upon Aeneas, second cousin of the now dead princes of Troy—including Hector, Paris, Deiphobus, Polydorus.

Juno despised Troy for several reasons.

From her great height, Juno also looked down upon her favorite city—Carthage—and dreaded the thought the descendants of Aeneas would someday ruin the now-fledgling town. If only she could stop Aeneas and end the prophecy concerning him.

Juno also despised the Trojans because her own daughter, Hebe, had been replaced as Jupiter's cupbearer. Her husband had chosen instead the Trojan, Catamitus (Greek Ganymede).

After the destruction of Troy, Aeneas had directed his ships to head west. Somewhere out there was a new home for him and his people.

Slowly, at first, and then with conviction, Juno descended down to Earth and to the island of Aeolus—master of the winds.

"My dear King Aeolus," said Juno.

"My goddess!" Aeolus stood back, amazed at her sudden entrance. "To what do I owe this honor."

Juno looked away for a moment, considering her words carefully, then turned back to him with a look that drilled into his eyes, commanding his full attention, even though she already had it. "I have come to ask a favor. A tiny thing, really. It's trivial, but it needs to be done."

"Yes, my lady?"

"I would like you to use your winds to create a storm. Over there," she pointed out to sea, "are the ships of Aeneas, the Trojan prince, and all his fellow refugees. I want them destroyed—especially the ship holding Aeneas."

"Hmm-mm," Aeolus nodded thoughtfully, then shook his head in disagreement. "My lady, I cannot. I have no grievance with Aeneas or his people."

"But you must," said Juno. "Perhaps I could make the task more attractive by including Deiopea to become your bride."

The king's eyebrows raised in appreciation of the offer. The sea nymph, Deiopea, was said to be the loveliest of all sea creatures. But he shook his head again. "My lady, I will not take her as wife, for I already have one, and she is sufficient for me. But because this means so much to you, I will help."

"Thank you, kind sir," said Juno, and abruptly vanished.

Immediately, Aeolus gathered all his winds and overwhelmed the Trojan fleet. This storm disturbed the surface of the sea, and suddenly, Neptune (Greek Poseidon) was alerted to the commotion in his realm.

"What goes on here?" Neptune demanded. He saw the winds and their target—the Trojan ships. The sea god had no love for Troy, but he resented the intrusion into his domain. "Be still, waters!" he commanded. And he calmed the winds, despite the efforts of Aeolus. This was Neptune's territory, and any intrusion by another god was unwelcome.

Neptune could smell the handiwork of Aeolus and knew someone else was behind this attack. Despite his dislike of the Trojans, he disliked the intrusion even more. So, he gave the ships of Aeneas a favorable breeze which took them to the north coast of Africa, not far from the new town of Carthage.

Aeneas and his fellow travelers landed on the shore, thankful to be alive.

In the distance, Aeneas saw a beautiful woman approaching on horseback. She had a bow strung across her shoulder and a quiver on her back. He watched her as she made her way to them.

"You are all lucky to be alive," said the woman, who happened to be his mother, Venus, in disguise. "Some of the gods favor you and your companions."

"I was beginning to lose hope," said Aeneas. "I appreciate your words, but even I was beginning to wonder if all of the gods might be against us, now that we have lost our war with the Greeks."

"Fear not," she said, "your destiny is to plant the seed of a great empire."

The young prince cocked his head to the side, uncertain he could believe this from some strange huntress on the beach of North Africa.

"And you are in luck," she said. "Not far this way," she pointed toward the West, "there is a new town called Carthage, founded by the Phoenicians of Tyre, and ruled over by good queen Dido. You will usually find her in the Temple of Juno."

"Well, thank you, fair stranger," said Aeneas, just as she prodded her horse into a trot in the same direction. "But—" and she was gone, receding into the distance, ignoring his words.

"I see trees over there, master," said one of his fellow travelers. "There may be a well and clean water."

"Good. Let's us refresh ourselves and then head toward this new town, Carthage."

Aeneas found his way to the Temple of Juno and there entreated the queen to help his small band of refugees. In the tradition of all civilized folk, she invited him and his fellow travelers to a banquet in their honor.

In the meantime, Venus met with her son, Cupid—half-brother to Aeneas.

"My darling son, I need your help. I would like you to help me create a bond between Queen Dido and your brother, Aeneas."

"Yes, mother."

At the banquet which Dido arranged for Aeneas and the other Trojans, Cupid showed up disguised as Ascanius, Aeneas's son by his first wife, Creusa. While the image of the son approached Queen Dido bearing gifts, invisible Venus surrounded the real Ascanius with a ghostly shroud to keep others from noticing there were two of him. Even the real Ascanius was bewitched into ignoring the imposter.

Dido graciously received the gifts and reached for the handsome young boy to draw him close. She felt an overpowering urge to give him a mother's affection. While in Dido's embrace, Cupid worked his charms on her, weakening a sacred pledge she had made to stay faithful to her dead husband, slain by her brother.

"Tell me, Aeneas," said Queen Dido, "all that has happened to you. I want to hear the entire story. Stories help us to understand." She was going to say that stories also entertain, but thought better of it, knowing the Trojan's tale would include great tragedy.

"Well, my lady," said Aeneas, "I would like to thank you for your gracious hospitality. We are weary from our travels. This spot of civilization soothes our souls."

The queen raised her cup toward him and smiled.

"Our once-great city," said Aeneas, "at the entrance to that enormous body of water, northeast of the Mediterranean—what the Greeks call the Euxine Sea—our city was attacked by the Greeks. For ten long years, they tried to destroy us all. Then, on the eve of what seemed like our victory, the Greeks left a gift on our doorstep and departed en masse. But the gift was our undoing, for within it was Greek soldiers who lay as still as death until we were drunk and asleep from our long celebration.

"By the end of the next day, our city was a smoldering mass of former humanity. Our people killed or under Greek subjugation. Some of us escaped inland. The next day, when the hostilities were done, and some semblance of peace returned, I went back to Troy to find my wife, but she was dead. In the smoke, I saw an image of her, and it spoke, telling me I would establish a great city to the West.

"Inspired by her words, I convinced my fellows to help me build our small fleet of ships. Our travels took us all over the Eastern Mediterranean—to Thrace, where we found the remains of our fellow Trojan, Polydorus. Then to Strophades, where we met Celaeno, the Harpy. She told us to leave her island. And before we left, she said I must look for a place called Italy. After that, we landed at Crete. We thought perhaps we arrived at our destination and began to build our city. We named it Pergamea. But then Apollo visited us and told us we had not yet arrived at our true destination.

"At fair Buthrotum, north of Macedonia, we attempted to replicate Troy. On that island, we met the widow of Prince Hector and found Prince Helenus who had also escaped. Now, Helenus has the gift of prophecy. From him, I learned more about my own destiny. He told me I needed to find Italy which is also known as Ausonia, and by the name Hesperia."

"There are two large peninsulas named Hesperia," said the queen. "One is due north of here, across the Tyrrhenian Sea. The other is at the far western end of the Mediterranean, north of the exit to our small, inland sea, and entrance to a far larger, Great Ocean, the realm of Atlas and the once great Atlantis which sank so long ago."

The queen suddenly felt self-conscious about what she had just said. The Phoenician custom was to keep secret the discoveries of the Phoenician people. Such discoveries were frequently made at great cost and to give them away would be to lose the Phoenician hold on such knowledge. But the queen had been feeling exceptionally joyous with the arrival of these guests. She felt overcome with a generous spirit.

"Thank you, my lady, for your help in our quest. After Buthrotum, we found ourselves in a land called Trinacria where our ships barely escaped a grave danger we later learned was called Charybdis—a vast whirlpool which threatened to swallow entire ships. From there, we encountered the Cyclopes and one of the Greeks—a soldier who had served under Ulysses—a soldier who had been left behind in their mad rush to escape the great, one-eyed beasts. We took Achaemenides, the Greek, on board with us, but barely escaped with our own lives when blind Polyphemus heard our voices. Not long afterward, my own father, Anchises, died peacefully of his own years. We sailed next into the open seas, unsure where to find this Hesperia—this Italy. A great storm nearly destroyed us, but then we found the coast not far from here."

"I am so thankful that you made it," said the queen. Her eyes glistened toward him, and at that moment, she knew she loved this prince.

Aeneas, too, could feel the bond and gazed upon her with deep admiration.

Later, after they had taken in their fill. Dido suggested Aeneas, and a few of his best hunters go inland with her to find game.

In the hall, but invisible to these mortals, Juno confronted Venus.

"Listen," said Juno. "I would like to strike a bargain with you. These two seem to be well-suited for one another. See how much they are in love?"

"Yes," said Venus, "what did you have in mind."

"I will stop my attacks on these Trojans if Aeneas stays here in Carthage with Dido, becoming her husband."

Venus smiled at the thought of her son marrying the local queen. This pleased her greatly. And since she already orchestrated the beginnings of love, she would do everything she could to hold Juno to her promise.

During their hunt, Dido and Aeneas followed their clues to find their prey and became separated from the others. And when a storm struck they found a nearby cave for shelter. Within the cave, Aeneas held Dido close to keep her warm. In that embrace, there came kisses and a deeper, more passionate experience which Dido took to mean Aeneas was now bound to her for life.

After they returned to the palace in Carthage, the two were clearly and deeply in love. But their affection was short-lived. While the two were together in her chamber, a bright light appeared in the middle of the room and suddenly there appeared the form of Mercury, messenger of the gods.

"Aeneas, son of Venus," said Mercury, "this has gone too far, and Jupiter himself has commanded me to intervene. You have a destiny, and it must be seen through to the end."

"But," said Dido. "does he have to stay away. Can't he return to me?"

"I'm afraid not, my lady," replied Mercury. "The future fate of the world hangs on the shoulders of Aeneas."

Dido shook her head and screamed in agony. The pain of such fresh love being snuffed out before its full blossom was too much to bear. She looked to Aeneas for some relief from her agony.

"Sorry, my love," was all he could say.

Her screams filled the palace with such remorse all could feel her pain.

Immediately, she grabbed the sword of Aeneas and left the room.

Cautiously, he followed. He could hear her commands to build a pyre in the great opening in front of the palace. When it had been built, she climbed up to the top of it, his sword in her hand.

"People of Carthage. We've all suffered too much tragedy of late. First, the murder of my husband, and now this tragic love that must never be. Suddenly, she plunged the sword into her abdomen.

Her eyes goggled in incredible pain, and she dropped to her knees, the sword sliding from her wound. "There will forever be great strife between our peoples, Aeneas. You have wounded me more than this sword could ever do." She then fell backward onto the pyre, gasping these final words, "rise up from my bones, avenging spirit."

Understanding the gravity of this act, Aeneas quickly gathered his people and ushered them out of the city and back to their ships.

As they sailed away, he looked back at Carthage, but all he could see was the smoke pouring upward into the sky from Dido's funeral pyre.

What History and an Analysis of Myth Tell Us

Estimates for the founding of Carthage range from 1215 to 814 BC. Modern historians seem to favor the later date, because of a reference made by Timaeus of Taormina that Carthage had been founded 38 years before the first Olympiad (776 BC). This is ironic and possibly quite wrong, if we believe the story of Aeneas, because the Trojan War was supposedly far earlier—traditionally dated at 1184 BC. Some historians placed the founding of Gadir (Roman Gādēs, Moorish Qādis, modern Cádiz, Spain) at about 1104 BC, as a colony of Tyre—far beyond Carthage when traveling from Tyre. While it's entirely possible that Tyre bypassed many locations to establish a lonely outpost beyond the far, opposite end of the Mediterranean, it seems more likely they created at least one or two intermediate colonies across that 4,000-kilometer length. The archaeological level at Hissarlik, Turkey, associated with the Trojan War, called Troy VIIa was destroyed about 1220 BC.

Though Aeneas has minor mention in Homer's *Iliad* the myth of Aeneas being the grandfather of Rome came about during the first century with writers like Virgil, Ovid, and

Livy. So, it seems highly probable the Roman connection to Troy, was contrived to establish a pseudo-historical basis for the Julian family brand.

From this fictionalized narrative, Julius Caesar could claim direct descent from the goddess Venus, through her son, the Trojan Aeneas. In addition, Aeneas's father, Anchises, was fourth grandson of Zeus and Electra. Thus, every time a member of the Caesar family spoke, they were speaking from a position of divine power, and this helped them to command greater respect. It didn't save Julius Caesar from the conspiracy to assassinate him, but it did help to lay the foundation of "gravitas" that grew into the office of emperor.

Venus was the goddess of love, but Julius Caesar had made a name for himself, and his extended family, more from his own acts of war—against the Celtic Gauls, and later against disruptive elements within the Roman Republic.

From these histories (contrived or handed down), we learn which gods favored the Romans and their founders.

Some of the other gods were no friend to Rome and its founding. These defacto enemies of Troy, and thus, by implication, of Rome, were Juno (Greek Hera), Vulcan (Hephaestus), Mercury (Hermes), Neptune (Poseidon), Thetis (no counterpart in Roman mythology), Timorus (Phobos), Formido (Deimos) and Discordia (Eris). Discordia (Eris), after all, was the goddess who had started the entire Trojan problem with her jealous spitefulness for not being invited to a divine wedding. It seems doubly abusive she should be against the party being attacked because of her own behavior. Supporting Troy, and by inference, also Rome, were Venus (Aphrodite), Apollo, Mars (Ares), Diana (Artemis), Latona (Leto) and Greek Scamander (no Roman equivalent).

From the expanded story of Aeneas, by the Romans, we see Jupiter also supported the Roman cause.

From Aeneas, the son of Venus down to the founders of Rome—Romulus and Remus—there were 15 generations of Latins, first at Lavinium and then at Alba Longa.

In the next chapter, we see how these divine, Trojan demigods struggled to establish a beachhead in the middle of the Italian peninsula, amongst numerous other tribes.

Chapter 2 — Founding of Rome

"Numitor is the rightful king," said someone in the crowd.

"Then why did he make it so easy for his brother, Amulius, to depose him?" asked Domitianus, "Does it sound right that such a reckless and weak king should remain on the throne? Numitor is too soft."

"If I steal your cloak," asked Remus, "does that make me the new owner?"

"If you were weak enough with your protection of your own property to permit its theft, then, yes," said Domitianus, "you would no longer deserve it." Remus did not miss the fact that his opponent had shifted the focus from Domitianus to Remus, apparently incapable of considering himself ever to be vulnerable.

"And," Remus raised a small purse of coins, "this used to be on your person, but you could not feel it when I took it? Does that make you weak and soft?"

"Give that back," said Domitianus reaching out for it.

"Why?" asked Remus. "It's mine, now. You said so in your own words."

Domitianus clenched his fists, furrowing his brow, and worked his mouth as if chewing a tough slab of beef. He stepped toward Remus, but one of his friends held him to keep him from taking another.

"Remus has a point," said Romulus. "Amulius stole the throne by force—betrayal from within. If I were Numitor,

I'd have Amulius drawn and hanged by his own entrails for his betrayal. Simple treason. You don't do that to your own king. Betrayal is one of the worst of crimes."

Remus continued to taunt Domitianus by dangling the coin purse in front of him. Suddenly, Remus attempted an underhanded toss which was poorly aimed—not with conscious intent—and hit Domitianus in the face with his own purse.

Enraged, Domitianus attacked Remus and the violence quickly spread throughout the crowd.

Romulus called for his supporters to withdraw. "Retreat, my friends. These traitors are not worth our time."

So, they departed, fending off the last few blows from their opposition.

When Romulus and his friends had retreated to a safe distance, they noticed the supporters of King Amulius also retreating, carrying their wounded.

"Where's Remus?" asked Romulus. He looked from one friend to another. They shrugged. "By the gods! They've taken my brother!"

"What do we do?" asked someone nearby.

"We rescue him," replied Romulus, sharply.

"Yes, yes. Of course," said another. "But how?"

"Iulianus, follow them," said Romulus. "Find out where they're holding my brother and report back."

The young man—their fastest runner—nodded and took off after the supporters of the usurper. Romulus spent the next hour gathering men to support a rescue effort. Not long afterward, Iulianus reported back and gave the location where Remus was being held.

Minutes later, three groups of Numitor's supporters approached the holding place by different paths and quickly overwhelmed the guards standing outside. Two others had been taken with Remus and all three of them were freed.

That evening, both Romulus and Remus received word King Amulius was looking for them. This was followed shortly by a message which took them both by surprise. It was from Numitor himself. He wanted to meet the two young men.

It was late in the evening when Romulus and Remus were led to the home of Numitor, the deposed king.

"Welcome, lads. Please," he motioned toward seats in front of a table toward the center of the room. "I have enquired about your family. Faustulus informs me that he found you both being suckled by a woman of the Rasennan wolf clan, not far north of here. She gave you two up to him, for she had merely found you both drifting on a raft on the River Tiber."

"Yes," replied Romulus. "That is as much as we know."

Numitor nodded. "I heard how you stood up for me against the supporters of my brother." He smiled.

"I am surprised," said Romulus, "that your brother would let you live after taking your throne."

"Yes," said Numitor, smiled weakly and turned from them, continuing to speak. "He has my daughter, Rhea Silvia, in a convent which they control. After Amulius led his forces to overthrow me, he had my son killed, and had my daughter committed to 30 years of celibacy in the convent to ensure I could not have an heir." Numitor nodded and turned back to them. "My brother fears me, but cannot kill me. It's ironic he can kill babies, though. He killed his nephew easily enough. But perhaps he feels it's safer to keep me alive so my supporters don't kill him outright."

"If only there were something we could do," said Remus.

"Perhaps there is," said the former king. "Perhaps there is. But first, let me tell you a story. Do you know of Aeneas?"

"Yes, of course," said Romulus. "Every child of our tribe learns of the great Trojan, descended from the gods—from Venus directly, as her son, and from Jupiter through his father, the fifth great-grandson of Jupiter, himself."

"Many of us," said Numitor, "are directly related to Aeneas and to the gods. When my daughter was locked away in the convent, Mars visited her."

"Really?" asked Remus. "In a convent?"

"He is a god," said Romulus.

"And my lovely Rhea has divinity running through her veins, just as it does through those of my brother. But she gave birth to twins." Numitor paused for a moment, looking deeply in the eyes of Remus, and then Romulus. "Amulius ordered those twins to be killed, but the servants put them in a basket and set them adrift on the River Tiber."

Romulus's eyes went wide, and he looked at Remus, who was equally surprised. "But—"

"When Aeneas reached these shores," continued Numitor, "he made friends with King Latinus of the Latins. The king was so impressed by the Trojan that he offered him his daughter, Lavinia, in marriage. This did not sit well with King Turnus of the Rutuli, for he had expected Lavinia's hand in marriage. Turnus therefore attacked, but Aeneas prevailed and killed Turnus. Aeneas founded the city of Lavinium, named in honor of his new wife.

"After the death of Aeneas, his son, Ascanius—also known as Iulus—became the king of Lavinium. A greedy Etruscan king, named Mezentius, attacked after Ascanius's installation as king, forcing the people of Aeneas to pay tribute. Not long afterward, Ascanius attacked Mezentius, killing his son, and forced the Etruscan to pay tribute. When that had been settled, Ascanius left the city under rule of his step-mother, Lavinia, and he went on to found this city of Alba Longa."

"But wait," said Romulus, "What was that you said earlier about twins and the river?"

Numitor smiled and nodded. "I am the twelfth great-grandson of Aeneas and you, my two wonderful boys, are the fourteenth great grandsons of Aeneas."

Both young men stood and again looked at one another. Numitor stepped toward them and flung his arms around them both, drawing them close for a strong embrace. "You are my grandchildren," he said. "I knew it the moment I heard of your strength of character, your support of me. You have the blood of the gods running in your veins." He stopped and wept, holding them tightly. They both embraced their grandfather.

Through the night, they talked about how to restore Numitor to the throne. Within three days, they had gathered the necessary forces and developed the strategy to overthrow Amulius, while also protecting their mother, Rhea Silvia. In the fighting, Amulius was killed along with many of his supporters. Those who were left were told to submit to Numitor or to face exile.

Both boys wished their grandfather well, but felt their destiny lay back where the Etruscan wolf woman had nurtured them. They returned to the seven hills of their upbringing vowing to build an even greater city. With their grandfather's blessings, they returned to the home they knew.

"There," said Romulus, "on the Palatine Hill. That is the most strategically defensible position for a new city."

"I disagree," said Remus. He pointed, "There, on the Aventine Hill."

They argued for several minutes, finally deciding to let the gods help in their decision.

"Let augury help us," recommended Remus.

"Agreed," replied Romulus. "Begin!"

"There, there, there," said Remus excitedly. "I have spotted six auspicious birds.

Romulus grumbled and waved for his brother to be patient. A few moments later, he said, "Well, now. Look at that. Twelve. I win."

"But I spotted mine first," said Remus. "I win."

Romulus shook his head and muttered, "Incredible. Do what you must. I'm building my city there." Again, he pointed to the Palatine Hill and waved to his followers. "Let's go."

Remus looked back to those who remained with him. "To the Aventine Hill," he said. "Perhaps we'll have two cities in support of each other."

Before long, Romulus and his men had built a wall partway around their new city. Remus decided to investigate the defenses and leaped over the wall. A surprised guard whirled on him and thrust his sword into the young man before the guard recognized who it was.

"By the gods," remarked Romulus, "what have you done?" He rushed forward and held his brother in his arms. "Remus, oh Remus!" The life went out of him and Romulus wailed with grief.

For several days, his men, combined with those who had followed Remus, continued to build the wall. Romulus, however, stood apart from them, working through his grief.

Finally, he gathered his men together to talk with them.

"This city has one major problem."

"But sir," said one of his men, "what could that be. The site is good," he looked to some of the men who had followed Remus, "perhaps as good as the Aventine Hill, and our wall is sturdy and highly defensible. What are we missing?"

Romulus chuckled and then smiled for the first time in over a week. "As we are now, we are a city of only one generation. After we are gone, so will be our city."

"What?"

"Oh," said one of the others. "Of course. No women."

Suddenly, everyone laughed.

"What I propose," said Romulus, "is that we negotiate with the Sabines just beyond these hills and ask for their daughters in marriage."

Everyone nodded. It sounded like a good plan, but when the Sabine elders were consulted, their answer was a resounding "No!" Those elders feared the competition. A new city-state in their midst could only mean eventual tyranny, overthrow, or conquest.

Though his men were disheartened, Romulus, smiled a sly grin as he gathered them once again to discuss their options.

"Men," said Romulus, "we have great skills—building, metallurgy, farming and the like. We, therefore, should be able to come up with a plan to gain the women we need. I propose that we prepare a feast and invite our neighbors to join us. Let us finish our wall, and use that as a guise for the celebration. We need weapons, but we also need food. We need to plan this carefully so that it is both enticing to our neighbors and foolproof in our aims to gain our future wives. In a few weeks, about the time we will be finishing our wall, there is the festival of Neptune Equester—god of the sea as patron of horses. We should have some horses by then, too."

Everyone nodded. And Romulus set them each to the tasks in preparation for their upcoming festival.

On the day of the feast, people from all the neighboring villages came—Sabines, Caeninenses, Crustumini, and Antemnates—bringing their sons and daughters to help the new Romulans consecrate their new city and to celebrate the completion of the outer wall.

Midway through the festivities, Romulus gave the signal and half his men grabbed a woman and took her forcefully back up to the wall. There, some of the men remained to guard their catch and keep them from escaping, while others used their new weapons to fend off the angry fathers and brothers. Then, more of the men grabbed another batch of young women to take to their wall, so all would have wives.

Only a small force was needed to guard the women. Most of Romulus' forces were employed to defeat the neighboring men and their wives, forcing them to retreat.

After the guests left, the kidnapped women were taken, one by one, to see Romulus. He talked to each of them, pleading with them to submit to their new husbands for the sake of their new civilization. He appealed to their maternal instincts, suggesting there is nothing more sacred than to share in the creation of children.

The next day, the King of the Caeninenses brought his army and attacked the Romulans. Their king was killed and their army was sent home, demoralized by their humiliating defeat.

Romulus gathered his strongest troops and attacked their city, Caenina, and easily took it. On the first of March, 752 BC, Romulus celebrated the defeat of the Caeninenses by dedicating ground for a temple to Jupiter.

The Antemnates attacked Romulus's new city. And again, Romulus retaliated, capturing their city. Then the Crustumini took up arms against the forces of Romulus and they, too, lost their town.

Finally, the Sabines decided Romulus needed to be vanquished for his theft of their women. King Titus Tatius sent his forces against the gates of the new city and found that one of the women would open the gates if she would receive what they wore on their arms. She was Tarpeia, daughter of Spurius Tarpeius. When she opened the gates, she was immediately killed by their advancing shields—borne on their arms--squeezing the life out of her. Her dead body was thrown off a nearby high rock which came to be known as the Tarpeian Rock—the place Rome executed all traitors.

Now, the Sabines held the city's citadel. The Romulans attacked but were easily repulsed. Romulus's men were depressed by their failure to reacquire their own city.

Romulus talked to them, attempting to lift their spirits. "By Jupiter himself, we will win this. And in his honor, I will build another temple, this time to Jupiter Stator. The gods are on our side if only we will do the brave thing and take these invaders down."

With his men sufficiently motivated, they attacked and sent the Sabine general running. As they closed in on their Sabine enemies, Romulus and his men received the shock of their lives.

Suddenly, between the opposing forces, the Sabine wives rushed to stop them.

"Hear me!" said one of the women, "oh men of Sabine and husbands of Romulus. We do not care to lose either our husbands or our fathers. Please, put down your arms, or you will have to use them against us. We cannot live without fathers or husbands. Please do not make us choose."

The war ended abruptly. King Titus Tatius agreed to rule with Romulus over both the new city and the old city of Sabinium.

As the final agreements had been made, one of Romulus' men spoke, "Sir, we have called this place our city or the city of Romulus, but we truly need a name worthy of a city. Perhaps we could call it simply, 'Romulus.'"

King Romulus looked down for a moment in all humility and then addressed first the man and then all his men. "My fellow countrymen. I am honored by this suggestion, but I would not want to forget my dear brother, Remus. Perhaps we can use his name, instead."

"Or," said another man, "we could use a shorter name that would remind us of both brothers—Roma."

Several others nodded or voiced approval of the new name.

"Yes," said Romulus. "This name makes me happy. I'm sure Remus would approve."

From the She-Wolf to the Founding of a Great City

The first time the story of Romulus and Remus appeared in Roman literature was toward the end of the third century BC. Whether their story had always been a part of the Roman culture is unknown. Many cultures had oral traditions that were eventually written down for posterity—the Greeks, the Germans, and the Romans.

Romulus and Remus were suckled by a she-wolf. The image seems to shout, "We are tough; don't mess with us." Modern scholars consider the wolf symbol to have been Etruscan (Rasennan). What might be more likely, if these two legendary heroes are based on real people, is they were suckled by an Etruscan maiden (human). Etruria (Rasenna), at the founding of Rome, included much of the surrounding terrain, with its capital at Velzna, northwest of Rome.

Many other cultures occupied what is today modern Italy. Modern-day Tuscany was home to the Etruscans, and in southern Italy and Sicily, Greeks occupied many places along the coast.

The tiny kingdom of Rome had a great deal of competition on the peninsula, including the two main islands associated with Italy: Sardinia and Sicily.

The city of Lavinium is, a real place, and archaeological evidence suggests Alba Longa was a real town or group of smaller towns along Lake Albano, stretching from the Alban Mount.

It took a great deal of practical, as well as military wisdom for the Romans to survive and to thrive amongst so many other cultures.

But the Romans had the gods on their side. Roman humility to the higher power of the gods made those mortals modest enough to seek practical and workable answers, instead of relying on their own, shortsighted egos.

Chapter 3 — Purely Roman Gods

Around 640 BC, King Ancus Marcius led his people down to the Tiber in a slow, solemn procession.

Ancus Marcius Rex, King of Roma, at age 37, had only recently become the tiny kingdom's new ruler. His predecessor was the grandson of Hostus Hostilius, the hero who fought alongside Romulus in reclaiming the city from the Sabines. Hostus died a hero, and his grandson made a fine king but paid too little attention to worship of the gods. Ancus was a Sabine by lineage, and grandson of the city's second king—Numa Pompilius—the great successor of Romulus.

As his first act, he ordered the Pontifex Maximus to make a public copy of the text of his grandfather's commentaries on religious rites, so every citizen knew the details of proper worship.

His people were soon intent on appeasing the god of the river—Tiberinus.

Four men carried a straw effigy of a man on their shoulders. They walked up to the edge of the water and waited.

"Citizens," said the king, "Let us first invoke Janus, the god of beginnings to bless this event so that everything we do here will have a righteous impact on our lives. Lord Janus, visit us now and consecrate these proceedings as only you can." He turned from one side to the other to survey the crowd, including them all in what he said.

"We gather today," the king continued, "to pay homage to Tiberinus and to his waters which bring life to the land. Please accept this offering of ours which symbolically links us to the river which bestows to us so many blessings every day of our existence."

A priest from one of the temples stepped forward and consecrated the straw effigy, saying several words of prayer over it. Then the four men threw the straw man into the river, and everyone watched as the current carried it toward the sea.

"Thank you, my good people," said the king, "and may the festivities begin."

There was a loud cheer from the crowd, and everyone walked back up the hill to where the eating and games were held.

Ennius Cloelius was an old man with white hair, but he walked erect despite his age. As counselor to the king, he was frequently found by the king's side. Today was no exception. As they walked behind the crowds of people, they talked.

"My Lord," said Ennius, "I've received reports that a number of the Latin tribes are becoming jealous of our successes. I fear they may attack."

"Thank you, my friend," replied the king, "It's always good to know the truth of things, even when bad news. We need to be prepared, certainly."

"But, Lord, how do we respond if they do attack?"

"With strength, certainly. We defend ourselves. But more than that, we need to realize the people of each city are not necessarily responsible for the acts of their rulers or their military. I, for one, would welcome more citizens, if they are willing to live in peace. As Romulus had done before us, we need to bring more of the Latins into our midst and give them a home within our protection. If more attack us, we defeat them, too, and take their citizens as booty—not as slaves, mind you, but as honored guests and citizens of our new nation."

"Thank you, my Lord. And how will we be legitimizing our attack on the Latins?"

The king laughed. "You're testing me?" He chuckled again and slapped the advisor on the back with affection. "As always, we consult the gods. We will only ever declare war on others through the rites of the fetials. After all, we do want to win, if we do go to war. The last thing we need is to attack and to find that the gods are against us in that attack. That would be foolish, indeed."

"I see, my Lord. Very wise."

"And, as always, my old friend, I rely on your wisdom to tell me when I need to rethink my case."

Earliest Rome

Rome had a habit of acquiring gods along with their conquest of territory and their peoples. The gods included here are those which inherently part of the Roman culture or were imported in the beginning when they kidnapped their Sabine brides.

Abundantia is the goddess of abundance and prosperity.

Bubona is the goddess of cattle.

Candelifera is the goddess of childbirth. The name literally means "she who bears the candle," perhaps referring to someone who provides light for deliveries made at night.

Carmenta is the goddess of childbirth and prophecy.

Clementia is the goddess of forgiveness and mercy.

Cloacina is the goddess of the sewers in Rome, and protector of sexual intercourse during marriage.

Deverra is the goddess of midwives and women in labor. The name means "to sweep away," and this is aimed at the evil that might threaten the mother or newborn child.

Dis Pater is the Roman god of prosperity derived from the land—minerals, metals, crops and more—and later of the underworld. How did the realm of the dead become associated with crops and minerals? Everything connected with the ground was also connected to the underworld. The dead were buried in the ground. Beyond the ground, as the old myths went, the gods ruled over the dead souls. Later, Dis Pater was absorbed into the god, Pluto, who was the counterpart to the Greek god of the underworld, Hades. Pater comes from the root for "father," and sometimes the god was merely called "Dis."

Edesia is the goddess of food who presided over banquets.

Fabulinus is the god of children and teaching them to speak. When an infant spoke their first word, an offering would be made to this god in thanks for the blessed event.

Felicitas is the goddess of good luck and success. Similar to Fortuna, but the luck coming from Felicitas was always positive.

Fides is the goddess of loyalty, trust, and good faith. Her symbol was the turtle-dove, and she oversaw the protection of all state treaties with foreign countries.

Honos is the god of military honors and chivalry.

Janus is the Roman god of beginnings, endings, and the doors or openings between states, realms, and conditions. We see his name even today in the Western calendar for the year's first month—January. Because everything important has a beginning, Janus was the first god consulted at such events—marriages, births, seasons, days, deaths, and even new buildings, and towns. All religious ceremonies had their beginnings. If a festival of Neptune were being held, Janus would be mentioned first, so the celebration begins on the right footing.

Romans held a fascination for omens. They were forever looking for signs to tell the future, and as the present passed through the doorway into the future, Janus was always present demanding consideration from each righteous Roman citizen. As the god of doors, Janus had some say about who could communicate with the other gods and was always consulted in matters concerning any divinity.

The god Janus likely derived from a conflation of two Etruscan gods—Ana (goddess of beginnings), and Aita (god of endings and the underworld).

Juventas is the goddess of youth, especially for the young men who have come of age and were "new to wearing the toga."

Lares was not the name of an individual god, but the term used for all personal, family gods. These gods looked out for the family, its members, and the spirits of its ancestors. Small offerings were given each day to the Lares so they would continue to take care of their dead ancestors and to look out for the good fortunes of the family. During more important functions, more elaborate offerings were made to the Lares in proportion to the importance of the event, whether it be a wedding, birth or some other occasion. See "Penates" for another group of protective gods. Roman cities had public Penates and Lares to protect them.

Larunda is the goddess of silence. She is famous for both her beauty and talkativeness. She was so loquacious she could never keep a secret. When Jupiter had an affair with a fellow nymph—Janus' wife Juturna—Larunda told Juno all the juicy details. For this betrayal of the King of gods to his wife, Jupiter cut out Larunda's tongue so she could never speak again, and Mercury escorted her to the underworld. Taken with her beauty, Mercury made love with her. To keep his affair with her a secret from Jupiter, Mercury hid her in a woodland cottage where the King of gods would never find her. The children she bore became known as the Lares. See also Muta and Tacita.

Liber and **Libera** are a pair of gods—male and female, who represented fertility. Liber was especially important in this patriarchal society as a symbol of male fertility, as well as the personal transition of a boy into manhood. The worship of Liber also involved partying. He was so popular early Romans dedicated an entire month to the adoration of this god. Celebrations included the symbol of male fertility—a giant phallic emblem which was paraded through the city to protect the current season's crops. Later, Liber was superseded by the Roman equivalent of Greek Dionysis, Bacchus. Liber was held in high esteem by traditionalist cults who desired to perpetuate the wild sex parties and the rare slaying of a partygoer which heightened the sense of pleasure.

Muta is the goddess of silence. Her name means "the mute one." See also Larunda and Tacita.

Ocnus is the Roman god of delay, hesitation, and frustration—everything to do with unsuccessful efforts, and is the son of Tiberinus. He was kept in the underworld, condemned forever to weave a rope made of straw. The rope was eaten by a donkey as fast as he made it, thus symbolizing the futility over which he had been given domain.

Penates, like Lares, was not the name of an individual god, but the term applied to all household gods. While the

Lares were protective, ancestral spirits, the Penates were gods of Roman households and guardians of storerooms and hearths. Roman cities had public Penates and Lares to protect them.

Pietas is the goddess of duty, loyalty, filial piety and proper religious behavior.

Pomona is the goddess of fruit trees, fruitful abundance, and orchards. She is a wood nymph.

Quirinus is an early Sabine addition. He is a god of war, long before Roman borrowed Greek Ares and renamed him, Mars. Later, when Mars was the defacto god of war, Quirinus became associated with Romulus, elevating the legendary founder to a form of divinity. Thus, Quirinus later represented Rome itself.

Sancus is the god of loyalty, honesty, and oaths.

Sors is the god of luck, possibly a son of Fortuna (see the chapter on Greek gods).

Spes is the goddess of hope.

Tacita is the goddess of silence. Her name means "the silent one." See also, Muta and Larunda.

Tempestes is the goddess of storms and sudden changes in weather.

Tiberinus is a Roman river god for the River Tiber, which ran through the capital city. Like many primitive societies, the Roman culture was at least partially animistic—viewing the world around them as possessing a dual nature—part physical and part spiritual. Tiberinus is the god who helped Aeneas when the Trojan first arrived in Italy. He suggested which allies should help Aeneas defeat the jealous Turnus who wanted Lavinia's hand in marriage. Tiberinus also rescued Rhea Silvia after her imprisonment in the convent. With a Greek female fortune teller named Manto, he had a son named Ocnus. Each 27 May citizens create a straw effigy and toss it into the Tiber River to appease Tiberinus.

Tranquillitas is the goddess of peace, calmness, security, and tranquility. Her qualities are the embodiment of the Roman Way (Via Romana) and the justification for Rome to subdue, overcome and civilize the world around them.

Trivia is the goddess of magic, witchcraft, sorcery. She often frequented graveyards and haunted crossroads. Only barking dogs could see her as she wandered about at night.

The Creatures of Roman Mythology

The Romans did not contribute much in the way of mythological creatures. Their attempts at creating these creatures for their mythological world seem weak compared to the efforts of the Greeks.

Achlis is an elk-like creature with an upper lip so large the creature grazed backward to prevent the lip covering its mouth. In addition, Achlis' back legs have no joints, so it cannot sit down, and remains standing while sleeping. Frequently, it would be found leaning against a tree while resting. Hunters took advantage of this defect by cutting halfway through the tree against which the creature leaned. When the creature's weight forced the tree to topple, the creature could not get up fast enough to escape the hunters.

Cacus is a fire-breathing giant who terrorizes the people who live around the Aventine Hill before Rome is built. Cacus is a son of Vulcan who loved to eat human flesh. He was killed by Hercules (Greek Herakles).

Caladrius is a snow-white bird that lives in the house of the king. In Greek myth, this bird is called Dhalion. The bird benefited the king's household as it served as it could absorb the sickness of anyone who fell ill.

Faun is half-human and half-goat. The top half is human except for horns on their heads. Sometimes, they would help humans; at other times, they would hinder them. Fauns are sometimes confused with Greek satyrs.

Genius is similar to the Greek Daemon—a generalized divinity associated with every individual person. Sometimes, this creature is compared to the soul. Every place also had a spirit or soul—the genius loci, or spirit of a place.

Lemures are vengeful spirits who have not been properly buried. They manifested as a formless darkness and dread.

Strix are birds of ill omen who feed on flesh and blood of men. They have long beaks, are golden in color, with black talons, and round yellow eyes. They also suckled their young, which indicates they may have been bats and not birds.

Tarpeian Rock is an object in Roman legend that created a sufficient amount of horror in the minds of its citizens. All Roman traitors were thrown from this rock to their deaths.

The Romans were not imaginative when it came to mythological creatures. In the chapter on Greek gods, we will also look at some of the Greek mythological creatures adopted by the Romans.

Chapter 4 — Borrowings from Etruria

"Okay, you're so smart," said Kutu Lausa, "tell us why our capital was named for Menrva Velzna, but the Greeks got it all wrong, thinking her name was Pallas Athena." He lifted his cup to his mouth and took another swig of wine.

Tarquin Pulenas squinted, held his cup aloft for a thoughtful moment, then gulped his remaining wine. Ramtha, his wife, quickly refilled his cup.

Leaning forward, Tarquin looked at his guest and replied, "Yes, I am smart, but also quite aware of our shared histories. Menrva left the capital of Pos—the head city—taking with her hundreds of fellow refugees. She also took with her the knowledge of a mature society, the elements of weaving, furniture making, shipbuilding, fishing and other things basic to the art of civilization. She was fully equipped with the armaments to protect her fragile group, and they set up their outpost on Sherden Island across the Rasna Sea. We Rasenna are direct descendants of those who followed Menrva.

"When she built her capital, she used all her wisdom to reestablish the foundation of civilization.

Her beloved, who she thought had been killed, was actually alive and joined her in building their capital. The people were so overjoyed their savior could benefit from some happiness of her own, they requested the town be named in his honor.

"In the language of the day, towns were called 'pels.' And, because his name was Aten, the town was given the name, Pel es Atenai—Town of Aten."

"But wait," said Kutu, "that name sounds somewhat Egyptian."

"Very good, my friend," replied Tarquin. "It wasn't Egyptian, but because Menrva and Aten befriended the Egyptians against the Sett, Aten's name made its way into their legends.

"To continue, ages after Pel es Atenai had succumbed to the rising seas, the children of Menrva's refugees spread across the world, and some settled in what is today is the Greek homeland. Kekropna was a general of our people, and he led his men to sit on the Acropolis of Athens, long before it received that name. There, they debated what to name their new city. But look—the focus was on the name of a city—not a person."

Kutu nodded and bit his lower lip thoughtfully.

"Okay, now look at this fact: Pel es Atenai looks very much like the name these ignorant, modern-day Greeks attribute to their goddess—Pallas Athenai—borrowed from us, though they think they originated the legend. It came from us through General Kekropna. But again, they were naming not a person, but a city. So, they gave it a city's name—Pel es Atenai.

"They debated between Athenai and another great city named Pos. By that time, they had conflated two cities which had good relations, even unto the time of Menrva—Pos, and Onn—but the two cities were not even close to the same location. Later, because of the nature of Pos, they used its name for their god of the sea—Poseidon—Pos and Onn.

"So, finally: Our capital was named Velzna—Menrva's family name in the ancient homeland toward the setting sun. Our people had left this area in an earlier age, traveling to Anatolia. But after our capital there was destroyed by the Greeks, we returned to our ancient homeland to start again."

Kutu took another sip and shook his head. "That's all well and good, and I appreciate you filling in a lot of the missing pieces for me, but I've also heard that Menrva's lover was, in truth, named Apollo, instead of Aten."

Tarquin laughed so hard, the bench upon which he sat shook, rattling against the floor. After a moment, he regained his composure enough to speak again.

First, he held up his right hand to prevent any interruption and took another swig of wine from the cup in his left. Again, he chuckled softly and then spoke. "Yes, I've heard that, too. And it's true. Yet, Menrva was faithful to her Aten until the very end. Some of today's young people condemn this notion of her having a dalliance with this other fellow, Apollo—god of the sun. But it's quite simple.

"In Egypt, Aten was god of the sun. And in his own land, to distinguish Aten from the town after which he had been named, the citizens gave him a nickname—a name which meant quite literally 'not the pel.' Can you guess?"

Kutu shook his head slowly, uncertain how to respond. "Apollo?" he asked weakly.

Tarquin chuckled again. "Yes, my friend. A-pel-u—not the pel. He was also Apollo, god of the sun, poetry, prophecy, medicine, and agriculture."

Now, it was Kutu's turn to laugh. He did so, shaking his head. "Amazing how simple things are when you know the whole story behind all of the various details handed down as scraps in one Rasennan family or another. Very good. Very good, indeed."

From Rasenna

The Romans knew them as Etruscans and called their land Etruria. Today, it's called Tuscany. The Greeks called them Tyrrhenians—the name used for the sea west of Rome. To the people themselves, they were known as Rasenna or Rasna.

The following are some gods and goddesses who made their way from the Etruscan pantheon to that of the Romans.

Libitina is thought to be an Etruscan goddess of death, corpses, and funerals. Some scholars believe the name is taken from the Etruscan root, lupu-, which means "to die."

Minerva (Etruscan Menrva) is the goddess of wisdom who took on the traits and history of the Greek goddess Pallas

Athena. As with Athena, Minerva was born from the head of Jupiter (Zeus) after the King of gods had swallowed her mother, Metis.

Orcus is the god of the underworld and punished those who did not live up to their oaths. Later, the Romans merged Orcus with Dis Pater, and then supplanted them with Pluto. Orcus provided the inspiration for J.R.R. Tolkien's orcs in his "Lord of the Rings" trilogy.

Volturnus is the god of water and the Tiber River. His festival is traditionally held on 27 August.

Chapter 5 — Influence of the Greek Pantheon

Flavius Secundus Iulius looked up at his father and frowned. After shaking his head for several seconds, he asked, "Why is it, father, that so many of our own gods sound like Greek gods? Not the names. No, that would be silly. But their descriptions—their attributes and accomplishments. Comparing Greek with Roman, they sound like the same gods, but with different names."

His father looked down at his son's large blue eyes and blond curls and smiled. He reached out and ruffled those curls, then winked.

Marcus Quintinus Iulius turned back to the plow shear he had been sharpening and continued to improve the blade with a sharpening stone.

"So?" said Flavius, as more of a demand than a question.

"Patience, my son," he replied, sliding the stone across the blade. "I'm thinking about the proper answer. You are wise to ask such a question, but not every answer will be so easily understood."

Flavius took a deep breath, let some of it out and said, "Yes, father."

The boy's slumped shoulders and down-turned mouth told his father the boy was not happy being patient. But even when the father had formulated an answer, he kept it to himself for several more, long seconds.

"Remember the hunt?" asked Marcus. "When you don't have patience..."

"...You can't catch game," Flavius repeated the well-worn lesson. He lifted his shoulders and let them down again, this time forcing them back. He sat more erect and compelled his lips to smile. "Yes, father."

Marcus laughed, a deep round noise that spoke of his pleasure with, and love of his son. "If you are in a crowd and someone your age calls out 'Iulius,' would you answer?"

"Possibly," he said, slowly, "if I were the only Iulius around."

"And," continued the father, "if someone else called out, 'Flavius,' would you answer them, as well?"

"In town, I suspect so," he replied, "since I'm the only Flavius that I know of."

"Fair enough." He gave his plow one more swipe with the sharpening stone, looked at the edge carefully and then set both the plow and the stone to one side. He turned to face his son squarely. "So, you would answer to two different names. And don't you have a nickname?"

"Father! Of course, I do. You've used it many times."

"Yes, I have. And it's a good one—Lex—meaning law or legal. So often you sound much like a legislator, with your logic. I'm proud of you, son."

Flavius nodded and looked away, suddenly distracted by his mother finishing the preparation for supper.

"So, Flavius Secundus Iulius Lex, you have a number of names that anyone could use to gain your attention."

"Yes, father. Even Secundus, on occasion."

"Very good. Now, the gods are very real. They have made their presence known to us, to the Greeks, to the Etruscans, and to many others, and they also have many names. To the Greeks, the founder of our family had the blood of Aphrodite flowing in his veins. To us, we call her 'Venus.' The goddess is the same. Different peoples merely have different names by which to call her."

Flavius nodded slowly, then hopped off his stool. Suddenly, he started pacing back and forth, hands tightly clasped behind his back. Then he stopped and stroked his chin, holding his elbow with his other hand, much as he had seen many a senator do in the capital. "So, Minerva is Athena; Jupiter is Zeus; Juno is Hera; Neptune is Poseidon, and Vulcan is Hephaestus."

His father nodded slowly and with a shallow, but certain movement. "We may not understand everything that the gods do, but if we uphold the nineteen virtues, that is the most the gods or any man can expect of us."

From the Greeks

Many of the gods we easily recognize as Roman may have been early Roman gods, but we have little documentation about them. Nearly everything we know about the following

Roman gods has been intermingled with the stories and traits of their Greek counterparts.

Jupiter (Zeus) is king of the gods--God of sky, lightning, and thunder. He is the patron god of the Roman state. His nickname was Jove.

Juno (Hera) is the queen of the gods, wife, and sister to Jupiter, and sister to Neptune and Pluto, and protector of the Roman state. The month of June was named after her.

Minerva (Athena) is the goddess of wisdom. She was originally an Etruscan goddess but was given virtually all the attributes possessed by Athena—the ones that she did not already possess in Etruscan myth.

Neptune (Poseidon) is the god of the sea, horses, and earthquakes.

Pluto (Hades) is the god of the underworld and ruler of the dead.

Caelus (Uranus or Ouranos) is the god of the heavens.

Saturn (Cronus) is the god of time and harvests.

Vesta (Hestia) was the virgin goddess of home, hearth, and family.

Apollo (Apollo), son of Jupiter and Leto, twin brother of Diana, and god of music, archery, healing, light, truth, and prophecy. He was responsible for taking the sun across the sky.

Bacchus (Dionysus) is the god of grape harvesting, winemaking, wine, fertility, theater, religious ecstasy, and ritual madness. His followers were many, because of the emotional and drug-like hook of alcohol consumption and the enjoyable revelry of partying.

Ceres (Demeter) goddess of grain, agriculture, crops, initiation, civilization. She is the protector of motherhood, women, and marriage.

Cupid (Eros) is the god of desire, attraction, affection, and erotic love.

Diana (Artemis) is the goddess of fertility, the Moon, hunting, nature, childbirth, forests, animals, mountains, and women. She is a guardian of creatures.

Discordia (Eris) is the goddess of discord and strife. It was because of her the Trojan War happened, and Aeneas ended up in Italy.

Hercules (Herakles) is a demi-god or divine hero who had incredible strength and used his unique abilities on many incredible quests.

Latona (Leto) is a goddess, daughter of the Titans Coeus and Phoebe, consort of Zeus and mother of the twins, Apollo and Artemis. Because Juno (Hera) was extremely jealous of her husband's girlfriends and their children, the queen of the gods forbade any land from receiving Latona so she could give birth. Ultimately, she found an island which was not attached to the sea floor—technically not "land"—and thereupon gave birth to the divine twins.

Mars (Ares) was, early on, a god of agriculture, but then took on the responsibilities as the god of war. He is also the father of Romulus and Remus—founders of Rome.

Mercury (Hermes) is a god with many responsibilities, including, commerce, financial gain, messages, communication, eloquence in communication, poetry, divination, travelers, boundaries, thieves, trickery, and luck.

Proserpina (Persophone) is the goddess of grain and Queen of the dead. She is the daughter of Ceres. She was kidnapped by Pluto and forced into living in the underworld for a portion of the year. We have seasons because everything died when she was underground.

Venus (Aphrodite) is the goddess of mortal love. According to myth, she was born of sea foam created by the severed genitals of Uranus that his son Cronus threw into the sea.

Vulcan (Hephaestus) is the god of fire and metallurgy. He is frequently seen with his blacksmith's hammer. In fact, when Jupiter had a splitting headache, years after swallowing Metis whole, Vulcan used his hammer to whack Jupiter on the head, thus splitting the king's skull and allowing Minerva to step forth, full-grown (mature), and fully armored, holding weapons at the ready.

Lesser Gods and Goddesses

The following lesser-known gods and goddesses were the Roman version of the Greek deity.

Aesculapius (Asclepius) god of health and medicine.

Aurora (Eos) goddess of the dawn.

Concordia (Harmonia) goddess of agreement in marriage and society. She was frequently associated with Pax ("peace") and thus remained symbolic of a stable society.

Fama (Pheme) goddess of fame and rumor. If you were on her good side, you received renown and notability. If you ever made her angry, you were more likely to be plagued by scandalous rumor.

Faunus (Pan) horned god of animals, forest, plains, and fields. His wife was called Fauna, and she had similar attributes.

Flora (Chloris) a Sabine goddess of flowers and spring.

Formido (Deimos) god of dread or terror. See also Timorus. Both Formido and Timorus had their Greek versions used as the names of the planet Mars's two moons. After all, horror and dread are two common emotions felt during war, of which Mars was the god.

Fortuna (Tyche) goddess of fortune and luck. She is similar to Felicitas, but luck coming from Fortuna could sometimes be very negative.

Hespera (Hesperides) goddess of dusk. In Greek mythology, the name used refers to a group of evening nymphs and sunset's golden light.

Invidia (Nemesis, Rhamnusia or Adrasteia ["the inescapable"]) goddess of revenge, envy, jealousy, and retribution, especially against those who unwisely became arrogant—confident without humility—in the face of the gods.

Iris (Iris) goddess of the rainbow and a messenger of the gods.

Justitia (Themis or Dike) goddess of justice.

Luna (Selene) goddess of the Moon. In Roman mythology, both Juno and Diana were considered moon goddesses, and sometimes "Luna" was used not as a separate goddess, but as an epithet applied to the multi-talented Juno and Diana.

Maia (Maia) goddess of growth and the oldest of the seven sisters of the Pleiades.

Necessitas (Ananke) goddess of destiny, necessity, compulsion, and inevitability.

Opis (Rhea) goddess of fertility, named after the Sabine goddess, Ops. She was said to be the wife of Saturn and mother of the chief Roman gods—Jupiter, Neptune, Pluto, Juno, Ceres, and Vesta.

Pax (Eirene) goddess of peace.

Portunes (Palaemon) god of keys, doors, ports, and livestock. Some scholars believe he may also have been associated with warehouses where the Romans stored their grain. The connection to ports likely came from the similarity between the Latin words "portus" (harbor) and "porta" (door or gate). Harbors were, after all, gateways to the sea.

Sol (Helios) god of the sun. An early form of this god was called Sol Indiges. The later form, Sol Invictus ("unconquered sun"), seems to have come from Mithraic influences during the Roman Empire, especially after 274 AD.

Somnus (Hypnos) god of sleep.

Timorus (Phobos) god of fear or horror. See also Formido. Both Formido and Timorus had their Greek versions used as the names of the planet Mars's two moons. After all, horror and dread are two common emotions felt during war, of which Mars was the god.

Veritas (Aletheia) goddess of virtue and truth.

Victoria (Nike) goddess of victory.

Voluptas (Hedone) goddess of sensual pleasure and delight.

Greek Creatures Adopted by the Romans

The following is a list of many of the more widely known monsters and other creatures of Roman myth, focusing on those imported from the Greeks.

Caucasian Eagle is a large bird which was destined to eat the liver of Prometheus every day while he was chained to one of the Caucasus mountains.

Centaur is a half-horse and half-man. In effect, it had two torsos and six limbs. Most centaurs of ancient myth were wild and uneducated, but Chiron was a wise centaur who taught many of the legendary Greek heroes.

Cerberus is a three-headed dog which guarded the gates of Hades.

Charybdis is a massive whirlpool at a narrow strait between the island of Trinacria (Sicily) and the mainland peninsula (Italy). The narrow strait was dangerous for ships. If it is a ship got too close to one side, it might be swallowed by Charybdis. If it got too close to the other side, its crew might be snatched up by the Scylla.

Chimera is a complex, hybrid creature which combined the entire body of a lion with a neck and head of a goat coming out of the middle of its back, and a tail with a snake's head on its end.

Colchian Dragon is a fierce reptilian creature which had a serpent-like head and body, plus wings and feet. It stood in the gardens of Colchis guarding the Golden Fleece. It was finally vanquished by Jason and his Argonauts with the help of the Colchian princess, Medea.

Cyclopes are giant creatures of man-like form, but with only one eye in the center of each of their foreheads. There were two groups of these creatures. The relationship between these groups remains unknown. One set of three Cyclopes was born to Caelus (Uranus) and Terra (Gaia). They were imprisoned in the underworld but were rescued and freed by Jupiter. They were so grateful they fashioned three gifts, one each for Jupiter and his two brothers. For Jupiter, they created a lightning bolt. For Neptune, they fashioned a magical trident. And for Pluto, they hammered out a helmet that imparted invisibility to the wearer. The other Cyclopes were children of Neptune. The most famous Cyclops of this group was Polyphemus who ate some of Odysseus' men and was later blinded by Odysseus and his fellow survivors.

Echidna is a goddess who was half-woman and half-snake. She is the wife of Typhon and the mother of many monsters.

Gorgons are three monstrous sisters who are sometimes pictured with wings. Stheno and Euryale were immortal, but Medusa was not (see also, Medusa).

Graeae is a group of three witches who shared a single eye through which they possessed psychic and clairvoyant sight. The Greek demi-god Perseus consulted them when he was on his quest.

Hydra of Lerna (also called the Lernaean Hydra, or simply Hydra). This is a many-headed snake, child of Typhon and Echidna. Some versions of the myth include the creature's ability to regenerate two heads for every one cut off. Both its breath and blood were poisonous.

Medusa is one of the Gorgon monsters. Because Neptune had raped Medusa in the temple of Minerva, the goddess of wisdom condemned Medusa with a special curse which turned her hair into living, venomous snakes and her gaze into one which could turn men into stone.

Minotaur has the head of a bull and the body of a man. He lived in a labyrinth beneath the Minoan palace. He was slain by Theseus, the Athenian hero and illegitimate son of the king.

Nemean Lion could not be killed by mortal men or their weapons. Its golden fur was impervious to common blades. Its claws were strong and sharp enough to cut right through armor, making the creature a dangerous, formidable opponent. He is the offspring of Typhon and Echidna. Hercules found the Nemean Lion living in a cave with two entrances. He blocked one entrance and then went in the other to confront the monster. In the darkness, he grasped the creature, and with his great strength, crushed the lion's neck, strangling it. To get proof of his conquest, Hercules attempted to skin the lion with his knife and then with a sharp rock, but neither one worked. Minerva saw his struggling and told him to use one of the lion's own claws to skin the beast which worked.

Scylla is a monster with six long necks, each equipped with a gruesome head with lots of sharp teeth. Her parents were Typhon and Echidna. She stood on one shore of the narrow strait between the island of Trinacria (Sicily) and the mainland peninsula (Italy), posing a danger to sailors. The narrow strait was dangerous for ships because if a ship got too close to one side, its crew might be snatched up by the Scylla. If it got too close to the other side, it might be swallowed by Charybdis (see Charybdis, also).

Sphinx is a creature with the head of a woman, the body of a lion, and the wings of an eagle. She blocked the road to travelers insisting they answer her riddle. If they answered incorrectly, she would devour them. When Greek tragic hero, Oedipus encountered the Sphinx, the riddle most often quoted went like this: "What is that which in the morning goeth upon four feet; upon two feet in the afternoon; and in the evening upon three?" Oedipus realized only a man does these things—first crawling on all fours as an infant, then walking on two legs as an adult, and finally using a cane as an old man. The Sphinx was so shocked someone had answered the riddle correctly; she devoured herself in her anguish.

Typhon is the son of Terra (Gaia) and Tartarus (Tartarus). He is the father, with Echidna, of many monsters. He challenged Jupiter for rule over the universe, after Jupiter, and his fellow gods had defeated the Titans.

Chapter 6 — Celtic Potpourri

Boudicca (30-61 AD) is a middle-aged woman of noble birth wronged by the Roman Empire.

Her late husband was King of the Iceni in Britannia. When he died, he left his kingdom to three parties—his two daughters and the Roman Emperor. But the Romans ignored the will because they believed women were not allowed to possess property.

Gaius Suetonius Paulinus, the Roman governor of the Empire's British holdings, simply annexed the Iceni territory. When Boudicca protested, she was flogged, and her daughters were raped.

But now, Governor Paulinus was away, claiming new territory for the Empire off the coast of Wales.

Behind Boudicca was a force of over 100,000 men and women, from her own tribe, from the Trinovantes, and from many others.

She wiped her upper lip, carefully with the back of her hand. Exertion and this sweltering, summer had her sweating profusely. Britannia during the Roman Warm Period was measurably warmer than in modern times. She lightly touched the gold torc wrapped around her neck—a symbol of royal authority amongst her people. The rigid neck ring was intricately decorated with symbols representing the spirits. On the front of her torc, where the two ends met, one end was embossed with the tiny image of three women—the máthair or matronae. The other end had embossed a tiny image of Epona—the horse goddess, and goddess of fertility.

She should not have to fight to restore the birthright of her two daughters, but they had been cheated by the patriarchal Romans. But here she was, leading a massive army toward Londinum—a settlement only 20 years old. Her forces destroyed Camulodunum, a Roman settlement that was rebuilt and called Colchester.

She looked back as she heard the others approach. The old man was Haerviu—too long in years to live up to his name "battle worthy." He was an adviser of hers and surprisingly had survived the war so far.

Lugubelenus was a brash young man who had already made several advances against one of her daughters and fancied himself as a leader. What he lacked in wisdom he made up for with fierce skills as a warrior and a deep humility to the gods.

Teutorigos was the last to arrive. His name meant "ruler of the people," and he had great potential but little interest in such power. His brand of humility was not the righteous kind, but more of a weak lack of ambition. A worthy Celt needed to maintain strong confidence, but with a deep humility to the gods and their laws.

"By Epona," she whispered loudly. "What have you found out?"

"Londinum is empty," replied Teutorigos quietly. "They've abandoned it."

"Apparently, they did not think their auxiliary forces could hold the settlement," said Haerviu. "I sincerely doubt the liars merely had a change of heart and decided to honor the will of their supposed friend, the late king."

"We should burn the settlement, nonetheless." Lugubelenus glanced at Boudicca and lifted his chin a bit.

"For once, I agree with Lugubelenus," replied Boudicca. "Punish these thieves in every way we can, but more importantly, force them to spend time rebuilding, if they desire to keep this Londinum. If the gods smile on us, perhaps the Romans will get the idea that holding this island is too much trouble."

"May Cernunnos guide us," said Haerviu. "We don't do these things for our own selfish needs, but for the greater good of the natural world, of which we are a part."

"Well said, as always, Haerviu," replied Boudicca. "May the three mothers protect us in what we are about to do. Teutorigos, send our scouts to the West. Make certain the governor isn't going to surprise us. Lugubelenus, take ten thousand men into Londinum and set it ablaze."

"Yes, my queen," said Lugubelenus.

Despite their successes, so far, Boudicca secretly feared Roman power. With such a vast, organized empire, her people could easily be overwhelmed by their millions. She prayed to the gods her people would prevail. But sometimes prayer was not enough.

Roman Conquests of the Celts

The Romans kept running into Celtic peoples—from Gallia and Britannia to Illyrium and Galatia. Roman expansion meant they encountered the Celts on almost every front, for over three centuries.

The **Matres and Matronae** were, across most of the Celtic world, worshipped throughout the period of the Roman Empire. Almost always, they were depicted on altars and votive offerings as a group of three goddesses—the "mother" goddesses. These divine beings were similar in some respects to the dísir and the valkyries of Norse mythology, as well as the Fates of Greek mythology. Dea Matrona means "divine mother goddess" and this name was sometimes used in place of Matres and Matronae. Dea Matrona was also the source name for the river Marne in Gaul.

Toutatis is considered a tribal protector for the Celts of Gaul and Britain. In Roman Britain, finger rings with the initials "TOT" were common and were thought to refer to the god Toutatis. Some scholars believe the Romans associated Toutatis with their own Mercury. In fact, Julius Caesar said that "Mercury" was their most esteemed god and that images of him were to be found throughout the Celtic territory. To the Celtic "Mercury" were attributed the functions of "inventor of all the arts," protector of merchants and travelers, and the preeminent god for everything concerning commercial gain. Toutatis could have been one member of a triune god named Lugus.

Caesar studied the Celts intensely because he wanted to conquer them. He also mentioned that the Celts of Gaul paid homage to Apollo because he rid them of diseases. They honored Mars, who ruled over all the things of war. They revered Jupiter, who oversaw the heavens. And they honored Minerva, who remained patroness of handicrafts. Julius Caesar also mentioned the Celtic Gauls all claimed to be descended from Dīs Pater, which was a Roman god of the underworld. Likely what he meant was that the Gauls claimed to be from a god who resembled Dīs Pater in some way—perhaps a subterranean god associated with prosperity and fertility.

Aerecura (see Erecura).

Aisus (see Esus).

Alaunus is a god of healing and prophecy which are two of the traits held by Apollo, both in the Greek and Roman pantheons.

Alisanos may have been a mountain god or may have been related to the alder tree.

Andarta is a warrior goddess with evidence of her worship in Bern, Switzerland and in southern France.

Anextiomarus (female form, Anextiomara) has been associated with the Roman god Apollo, with dedications found throughout France and Switzerland.

Artio is a bear goddess. Her worship was centered on Bern, Switzerland.

Aveta is a mother goddess worshipped across a region which includes parts of France, Germany, and Switzerland.

Belenus is a sun god, associated with horses, and thought to ride across the sky in a horse-drawn chariot, pulling the sun along with it. His consort is Celtic goddess Belisama, who is frequently associated with Minerva.

Borvo is a god involved in healing, minerals, and bubbling spring water. Whenever associated with a Roman god, Borvo was always paired with Apollo.

Brigantia is associated with Roman Victoria and remains a cognate with Irish Brigit.

Camulus is another Celtic god associated with Mars. In one stone carving, he is portrayed with a wreath of oak. In another location, he is shown with a ram head wearing horns. His name may have been the basis of Camelot—the legendary city of King Arthur fame. Many theories have been offered about the possible reality of King Arthur, but there is no way to verify them with the current evidence.

Cathubodua is a Celtic goddess and possible cognate of Irish Babd Catha. Her name meant "battle crow." Several goddesses share the same root which means either "victory" or "fighting." Because of this, she would be comparable to goddesses in other cultures—Victoria (Roman), Nike (Greek) and Sigyn (Norse).

Cernunnos is a horned god of life, fertility, wealth, animals and the realm of the underworld. He is shown with stag antlers, sometimes carrying a coin purse. Most of the time he is seen seated cross-legged. He is also shown wearing torcs or holding them in his hands.

Cicolluis is the "Great-Breasted" god of strength, associated with Mars. This god has sometimes been associated with Cichol Gricenchos of Irish Celtic myth.

Cissonius is yet another Celtic god associated with Mercury. In attempting to understand his name, linguists have interpreted it as meaning "carriage-driver" or "courageous." From this, they suspect he is a god of trade and patron protector of those who traveled. Thus, the association with Mercury seems to be a good fit. There is also a minor note of a goddess named Cissonia, but the relationship to this god is unknown.

Condatis—a name which means "waters meet"—is a Celtic god related to rivers, especially where they come together. He is associated with the Roman god Mars, likely through his divine healing powers.

Damona is a Celtic goddess. According to one scholar, her name means "divine cow"—from Celtic "damos" which means "cow." In two different regions, she was seen with a divine consort—Apollo Borvo in one, and Apollo Moritasgus in another.

Epona is a goddess of fertility, plus a protector of horses, ponies, donkeys, and mules. The Roman spelling was sometimes Hippona. She was one of the most broadly worshipped of any Celtic god. Some scholars feel she may have been associated with the dead, leading them to the "otherworld" on a pony. Evidence of her worship has been found in Britain, throughout Gaul, modern Germany and the Roman provinces of the River Danube. One inscription in Germany was made by someone from the region of ancient Syria.

Erecura (also spelled Aerecura) a Celtic goddess associated with the Roman goddess of the underworld, Proserpina (Greek Persophone). Evidence of her worship has been found in modern Belgium, southeastern France, southwestern Germany, eastern Austria, northeastern Italy and central Romania. Along with her symbols of the underworld, she is frequently seen with a cornucopia or an apple basket—symbols of fertility. Though the Celts revered this goddess across a broad territory, scholars doubt the name was, in fact, Celtic. One researcher suggested the name was originally Illyrian.

Esus (also spelled Hesus and Aisus) is a Celtic god. He was depicted cutting branches from a willow tree with his blade. One intellectual suggests that his name derives from the Indo-European root for "well-being, passion, and energy." The willow tree may represent the "Tree of Life." He could have been one part of a triune God, Lugus.

Grannus is a Celtic god of spas—healing mineral and thermal springs. He was also associated with the sun, and thus frequently associated with Apollo as Apollo Grannus. His worship was also frequently associated with Celtic Sirona and sometimes Roman Mars. Perhaps the most famous center for worshipping Grannus can be found near the modern city of Aachen, Germany, that country's westernmost municipality. In ancient times, the hot springs there was called Aquae Granni. Roman Emperor Caracalla (AD 188–217) was said to have visited there with votive offerings and prayers to be healed.

Hesus (see Esus).

Ialonus Contrebis (or Ialonus and Gontrebis) was either a Celtic god or two gods. The first part—Ialonus—seems to come from a root meaning "clearing."

Lenus is the Celtic god of healing, frequently associated with Roman god Mars. He was particularly important to the Treveri tribe in what is now western Germany. Unlike most syncretized names combining Celtic with Roman divinity, most inscriptions show "Lenus Mars," rather than "Mars Lenus." Quite often, he is pictured wearing a Greek Corinthian helmet.

Litavis (also Litauis) is a Celtic goddess sometimes associated with the Gallo-Roman syncretized god, Mars Cicolluis, suggesting she may have been his consort. Some scholars consider her to be an earth goddess with a name derived from language roots meaning "to spread out flat."

Loucetios is a Celtic god whose name means "lightning." He was invariably associated with Mars as Mars Loucetios and frequently associated with the goddess Gallic Nemetona or Roman Victoria. He was known throughout the Rhine River Valley region, from Austria and Switzerland, through Germany, France, Liechtenstein and the Netherlands. Inscriptions to this god have also been found in Angers, western France and in Bath, England.

Lugus is a Celtic god whose name remains a cognate with the Irish god Lugh. Though his name is rarely mentioned directly, his importance is implied by the proliferation of place names which seem to pay homage to him. His name seems to come from the Proto-Indo-European roots "to break" and "to swear an oath." A three-headed image found in Paris and Reims was thought to represent Lugus and is associated with the Roman god Mercury. Linguists suggest his name was the basis for the following location names:

- Dinlleu, Wales
- Legnica, Silesia
- Leiden, Netherlands
- Lothian, Scotland
- Loudoun, Scotland
- Loudun and Montluçon in France
- Lugdunum (modern Lyon, France)
- Lugones, Asturias, Spain
- Luton, England

One scholar suggests Lugus was a triune God, as represented by the three-headed image, representing Esus, Toutatis, and Taranis.

Maponos is a Celtic god with a name that meant "great son." He was equated with Roman Apollo.

Mogons is a Celtic god frequently adopted by common Roman soldiers in Roman Britain and Gaul. Linguists suggest its meaning derives from roots for "effective" or "powerful."

Nantosuelta is a Celtic nature goddess of fire, earth, and fertility. She is thought to have been part of the Irish Tuatha Dé Danann, combined with Sucellus and subsequently with Dagda. Some evidence suggests hers was the name assumed by The Morrígan after a joining of new alliances or a transformation. Her name literally means, "sun-drenched valley" or "of winding stream."

Ogmios is a Celtic god of persuasiveness. His name remains a cognate with the Irish god Ogma. He is described as an older version of Herakles, the Greek demigod of great strength. Like Herakles, Ogmios wore a lion skin and carried a club and bow. In his Celtic version, however, he is seen with chains piercing his tongue, flowing from his mouth and out to the ears of his happy followers.

Ritona (also Pritona) was a Celtic goddess of "water crossings" or "fords." Her temples seemed to have more extras than do many of the other gods—like courtyards which could easily have been used for the placement of ritual offerings or the preparation of religious banquets. Another such temple even had a theater, supposedly for religious performances.

Rosmerta is a Celtic goddess of abundance and fertility. Her image is often found alongside the Roman god Mercury as if she were his consort. She was worshipped from central France to western Germany.

Segomo is a Celtic war god whose name meant "mighty one" or "victor." Naturally, he is associated with the Roman god, Mars, but also with Hercules.

Sirona is a Celtic goddess throughout Gaul but also worshipped as far east as the Danube River. She has been associated with the Roman goddess, Diana.

Sucellus is a Celtic god frequently depicted with Nantosuelta. He is usually seen carrying a large hammer or mallet, which could easily have been a beer barrel on a long pole.

Suleviae was a group of Celtic goddesses whose name meant "those who govern well." This group was sometimes associated with the Matres. In fact, one inscription starts out, "To the Sulevi mothers…"

Taranis is a Celtic god of thunder. One curious coincidence ties Taranis with the Greek cyclops Brontes (whose name meant "thunder") because both were associated with a wheel. Some scholars suggest that Taranis was not so much a god of thunder as he was actually the thunder itself. His worship spanned a broad territory including Gaul, Britain, parts of former Yugoslavia and modern Germany. Lucan, the Roman poet, called Taranis a "savage god" who required human sacrifice. Taranis also remains a cognate with the Irish god Tuirenn. Taranis could also have been part of a triune God, Lugus. Because of his association with thunder or identity as thunder, he is also associated with the Roman god Jupiter, the Greek god Zeus, and the Norse god Thor.

Virotutis is a Celtic byname given the Roman god, Apollo. It meant, "benefactor of humanity." Apollo Virotutis was worshipped just south of Switzerland and in western France.

Visucius is a Celtic god whose name meant "knowledgeable" or "of the ravens." He was usually associated with the Roman god, Mercury, and was worshipped from western Germany to northern Spain.

Other Borrowed Gods

One goddess which was actively sought out by the Romans was the Phrygian Great Mother, Cybele. The assimilation of this goddess had nothing to do with conquest. During the Second Punic War (218–201 BC), the Romans suffered one setback after another. Several natural events were taken as signs of imminent failure in their war against the Carthaginians. One of those signs was a meteor shower, which the ancients always took as a bad omen, even though their enemies were very likely to have seen the same sign. Another involved a failed harvest and resulting famine. But that was merely a natural occurrence of climate change, cooling the planet between warm periods. There was a particularly sharp drop in temperature, measured in the Greenland ice cores indicative of a northern hemisphere cooling period that lasted several years during the time of the Second Punic War. But despite these things, the Romans were persistent and insistent.

After consulting the Sibylline oracle, Rome's religious advisers came up with a unique answer to their problem. If they could legally import the Magna Mater (Cybele) of

Pessinos, Phrygia (west-central Anatolia, or modern-day Turkey), they would be able to regain the favor of the gods.

In Rome's favor, the home of worship of this "Great Mother," was at the center of one of their allies—the Kingdom of Pergamum.

Immediately, the Roman Senate sent emissaries to gain the king's approval for Rome to import the goddess. These emissaries stopped by the Oracle at Delphi to confirm they were doing the right thing and received the confirmation they sought—that the goddess should be taken back to Rome.

To make the transference official, the King of Pergamum gave his Roman friends a black meteoric stone which was symbolic of the goddess. In a great ceremony full of pomp, the stone was met at Rome's seaport at Ostia and escorted by Rome's "best man," Publius Cornelius Scipio Nasica, along with an entourage of virtuous matrons to take the stone back to the temple of Victoria to be stored, while a more rightful temple of the Great Mother was being built on the Palatine Hill.

Not long afterward, the famine ended, and the Romans were victorious against Hannibal and the Carthaginians.

One of the most important gods which the Romans borrowed from cultures other than the Etruscans, Greeks or Celts, was the Persian god, **Mithra**—renamed Mithras by the Greeks, and worshipped by Imperial soldiers. The citizens-at-large knew about the worship, but the adherents kept their rituals and prayers a secret. Roman Mithraism was a "mystery religion," full of symbolism and secrecy. They did not need or want new members. They had a special handshake, plus an intricate system of seven levels for the various stages of initiation. Some rituals involved the killing of a bull. To its adherents, each ritual symbolized the struggle between good and evil, and of the sacrifice that is sometimes required. Roman Mithraism presented strong competition for early Christianity.

In 312 AD, at the Battle of Milvian Bridge, Constantine the Great (c.272–337 AD) had a decisive win, the success of which he later attributed to the **Christian God.** After that battle, he converted to Christianity and placed the Christian God ahead of all others.

After nearly two centuries of brutal persecution, the Christian religion had become the dominant religion in the Roman Empire. Because of Constantine's conversion, Europe became predominantly Christian.

Chapter 7 — Truth Behind the Roman Gods

While we may never know the actual truth behind each Roman god and goddess, we should acknowledge there is some unknown truth that may well remain unrecorded by any history, as with any myth. What do we mean by this? At the very least, the gods may have been created to explain physical or social phenomena. This is one possibility.

Another possible truth is that a god or goddess may have been an ancient king, queen, hero or heroine.

Still another possibility holds that some of the gods and goddesses of myth were groups, instead of individuals. At least one other researcher has put forth this idea, and we should remain open to this possibility.

To primitive hunter-gatherers, the name of an empire might have been a mystery because they didn't have any concept of "empire." It's easy to see how such a name might have become transformed into a god or goddess. It's also easy to see how the many traits of a god may merely have been the talents collectively held by a group, especially if the hunter-gatherers suffered from the power of the empire.

For example, we trust those in authority. But for over a thousand years in Europe, those in authority did not consider challenging their ideas about the universe. Even today, non-traditional ideas are discounted, ignored, or even ridiculed simply because they don't fit some current consensus. Simply because an idea is popular doesn't make it right. For example, scientists of the 19th century felt Homer's *Iliad* was purely myth with little basis in fact.

Scientists felt that Troy was pure myth simply because they had known of no evidence to the contrary. While this conclusion from a lack of evidence is value, it should not present pursuing further exploration. The pursuit of evidence of Troy did, in fact, lead to the discovery of Troy.

It is possible that pursuit of the truth underlying myths could lead to challenges to the prevailing religious understanding.

As we saw earlier, the Etruscans have a genetic relationship to the people who currently live in what is modern Turkey (ancient Anatolia or Asia Minor). The Etruscans may have been descendants of Aeneas and the Trojans, or at least the people who lived in and around Troy, They may, therefore, have been distant relatives of Romulus and Remus. Was Etruscan the language of the Trojans, or a derivative of their language? As far as we know, the Trojans did not employ writing, so we cannot prove such an idea. But an inability to prove an idea doesn't make it false. It simply remains an unknown.

One researcher—Rod Martin, Jr.—discovered a linguistic link between Etruscan (Rasennan) and Basque (Eskual), albeit a weak one. The nature of the link suggests both cultures may have been matriarchal at one time. The most sentimentally favorite words in any language may arguably be "mother" and "father." Basque for father is "aita," while mother is "ama." Etruscan for father was "apa," while mother was "ati." This, by itself, seems very weak, indeed, and the terms seem to be gender opposites. But as we saw earlier, the Etruscan goddess of beginnings was "Ana," while the god of endings was "Aita." These match the Basque terms almost perfectly by gender.

Martin suggests both cultures may have been matriarchal in prehistory. As more patriarchal societies entered Europe, peer pressure may have affected a desire to switch.

"What? You let your women rule? You must be weak!" would be the attitude of a patriarchal society. If a patriarchal tribe judged a matriarchal society as weak, they might continue to attack that society. Weary of being attacked, a matriarchal society might switch to change the perception of their enemies.

Both Greek and Roman cultures viewed the Etruscans with disdain, even though the Etruscans were patriarchal because they gave their women so much power and allowed them to own property. But what if, instead, it was the women who gave their men the power?

In analyzing the two languages, Martin realized both were agglutinative. That by itself proves little. But he suggests the Basques switched to patriarchy and kept the terms for mother and father with the same gender always attached to those terms. However, the Etruscans kept the terms with the societal roles. Their rulers had been mothers and men became the new mothers—"apa," or two letter "a's" separated by a labial sound ("p"), just as Basque for mother—"ama"—is also two letter "a's" separated by the labial "m." The names of their god and goddess of endings and beginnings may hold the clue to the gender switch, because Basque for father, "aita," is exactly the same as the Etruscan male god for endings, "Aita." And Basque for mother, "ama," is almost the same as the Etruscan female goddess for beginnings, "Ana."

How valid is this analysis? Even Martin acknowledges this is a hypothesis which needs additional support. But one other culture may validate this notion of a matriarchal society switching to patriarchy and keeping the terms with the role rather than the gender. Another agglutinative language—Georgian (Kartuli ena)—may have experienced a similar phenomenon. Today, Georgian for mother is "deda," and father is "mama."

Georgia, at the eastern end of the Black Sea, was at one time called Colchis—the kingdom which held the Golden Fleece and a golden dragon to protect it. Were the Georgians related in some way to the Trojans, Etruscans, and therefore the Basques? Linguists of the 19th century felt the similarities between Basque and Georgia were strong enough to consider the possibility they were descended from the same tongue. Both regions have also been called "Iberia," even though they are separated by thousands of kilometers. As tantalizing as the possibilities are, we need to use restraint and remind ourselves we simply do not know. Today, linguists tell us the evidence linking the two languages is too tenuous to prove a link. But again, a lack of evidence is never proof against a thesis. It only means we need more evidence.

In the final analysis, we may never have conclusive answers to our questions of divine beginnings. The Roman family of gods was perhaps one of the largest of all ancient pantheons simply because they absorbed the gods and goddesses of the peoples they conquered.

But what about the creatures of myth. Was there some basis in reality for them, as well, or were they all based purely on imagination? Consider, for instance, what a primitive man might think of someone wearing a flight suit or astronaut's spacesuit. Would the faceplate of their helmet be thought of as "one eye," making them a Cyclops?

Some researchers believe centaurs were merely the result of primitive shock and awe at seeing a normal man riding horseback. In their imagination, they saw only the human torso and head, and horse body. Having never seen the combination of horse and rider, the primitive mind attempted to process the image in the only way it could—imagining they had witnessed a new kind of creature.

Could the faun merely have been a soldier with furry leggings and leather boots, wearing a helmet with horns? These are possibilities, but with no way to know for certain.

And such is the nature of any myth. Its beginnings remain shrouded in the mists of prehistory.

Conclusion - What We've Learned

I hope this book has helped you to gain a fresh perspective of the Romans and an overview of their gods, goddesses, and mythological creatures.

In the introduction, we learned that the Romans were a serious lot. Though they were not very creative, they did have many virtues, including the fact that they were hard working and were clever at using well the resources available to them. We learned that they were originally farmers and that their gods had a lot to do with rain and crops.

Chapter 1, "The Trojan Connection," gave us a look at Aeneas and how one goddess, in particular, hated the Trojan and the survivors of the Trojan War. We also gained historical context of the Roman myth of Aeneas.

In chapter 2, "Founding of Rome," we got an intimate look at the founding of that great city by Romulus and Remus. We also learned how tiny Rome was surrounded by dozens of other tribes, each vying for supremacy or merely trying to survive.

Chapter 3, "Purely Roman Gods," showed us the early Roman kingdom and the celebration of the river god, Tiberinus. We also saw a list of Roman gods, many of which were likely unfamiliar to the casual student of history. And we saw a few of the awkwardly unimaginative creatures from Roman myth.

In "Borrowings from Etruria" (chapter 4), we looked at the gods and goddesses contributed by Rome's vastly larger neighbor to the North—Rasenna, or as the Romans knew them—Etruria. Our narrative took a fanciful look at one possible interpretation for how the various pantheons may have fit together. We also saw how the Etruscans might have been more closely related to the Romans than we've been led to believe, with their ancestors possibly having come from Troy along with Aeneas. And we learned of a few gods and goddesses which contributed to the Roman pantheon.

Perhaps the greatest foreign contribution to Roman mythology came from the Greeks. In chapter 5, "Influence of the Greeks," we saw how nearly all of the most well-known Roman gods and goddess were largely Greek gods which were restyled as Roman. And we saw how the richest list of Roman mythical creatures was populated with names borrowed from the Greeks. This should not surprise us, for to the Romans, Greek myth had merely become part of their own history.

In chapter 6, we learned how the Celts contribute a great deal of their own mythology to the Romans. With the Celtic pantheon, Roman gods and goddesses now took on composite names which combined Roman and Celtic elements.

Finally, in chapter 7, we explored some of the possible origins of the gods and goddesses.

Can you help me?

If you enjoyed this book, then I'd really appreciate it if you would post a short review on Amazon. I read all the reviews myself so that I can continue to provide books that people want.

Thanks for your support!

Check out another book by Matt Clayton

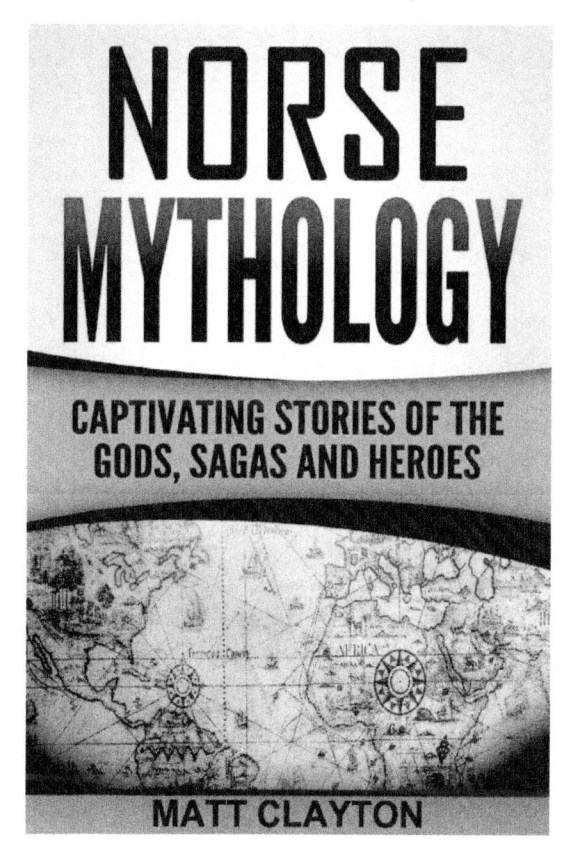

NORSE MYTHOLOGY

CAPTIVATING STORIES OF THE GODS, SAGAS AND HEROES

MATT CLAYTON

Free Bonus from Captivating History (Available for a Limited time)

Hi History Lovers!

Now you have a chance to join our exclusive history list so you can get your first history ebook for free as well as discounts and a potential to get more history books for free! Simply visit the link below to join.

Captivatinghistory.com/ebook

Also, make sure to follow us on:

Twitter: @Captivhistory

Facebook: Captivating History: @captivatinghistory

Printed in Great Britain
by Amazon